# SENSATIONAL SCIENCE ACTIVITIES

## = with DR. ZED =

### BY GORDON PENROSE
### ILLUSTRATED BY TINA HOLDCROFT

SIMON AND SCHUSTER BOOKS FOR YOUNG READERS
Published by Simon & Schuster Inc.
New York • London • Toronto • Sydney • Tokyo • Singapore

SIMON AND SCHUSTER
BOOKS FOR YOUNG READERS
Simon & Schuster Building
Rockefeller Center, 1230 Avenue of the Americas
New York, New York 10020

10 9 8 7 6 5 4 3 2 1      10 9 8 7 6 5 4 3 2 1 (pbk)

Library of Congress Cataloging-in-Publication Data
Penrose, Gordon. Sensational science activities with Dr. Zed.
Summary: Presents twenty-one projects which can be safely done
at home using readily available materials, demonstrating basic
scientific concepts, from physics to chemistry to biology.
1. Science—Experiments—Juvenile literature.   2. Scientific
recreations—Juvenile literature. [1. Science—Experiments.
2. Scientific recreations.   3. Experiments]   I. Holdcroft, Tina, ill.
II. Title.   Q164.P368   1990   507.8   90-9724
ISBN 0-671-72552-1      ISBN 0-671-72553-X  (pbk.)

Portions of this work were originally published in OWL magazine.

# CONTENTS

# DR. ZED'S CRAZY KAZOO

Replace waxed paper when it gets wrinkled. → cut hole — hum into here — elastic band

## How to make your Crazy Kazoo

**1.** Cut a dime-sized hole in the middle of the cardboard tube.

**2.** Cut a piece of waxed paper 10 x 10 cm (4 x 4 inches).

**3.** Stretch the waxed paper tightly over one end of the tube.

**4.** Fasten the waxed paper to the end of the tube with the elastic band. You might have to wrap the band around more than once to make sure it's tight enough.

**5.** Try different tube lengths and kinds of materials to hear what sounds they produce.

# DR. ZED'S BUBBLE CITY

## How to Make Your Bubble City

**1.** Mix the first three liquids together in one glass. Put water in the other glass.

**2.** First wet the surface you're going to work on with water, then thinly spread about two-thirds of the soap solution until you've made a puddle the size of a large pizza.

**3.** Dip the straw in water. Then put one end of the straw in the soapy puddle and blow gently into the other. N.B. You can build bubbles on bubbles or bubbles within bubbles. But make sure you dip your straw in water before you try to stick it through a bubble or the bubble may pop.

It's the glycerine that keeps the bubble from drying out.

Wow! That last bubble lasted 30 seconds.

**Things you'll need:**
50 mL (3 tbsp) water; 15 mL (1 tbsp) dish washing liquid (Joy works best); 15 mL (1 tbsp) glycerine; two drinking glasses; water; smooth surface; drinking straw

What did one bubble say to the other.

Just thought I'd pop by.

**About this experiment:**
Dr. Zed investigates surface tension in a soapy solution.

The soap makes the water more elastic - as though a rubber skin were stretched across the surface. When you blow air into the solution the skin stretches. The more soapy water and the more air, the bigger the bubble.

How do you get a bubble from a puddle of soapy water?

## How to Make Your Rocket Launcher

**1.** Cut the wide straw so it is 5 cm (2 inches) shorter than the narrow one.

**2.** Staple one end of the wide straw several times and seal this end with sticky tape to make it airtight.

**3.** Snip just enough off the tip of the paper cone so that the wide straw will fit through snugly. Tape the tip of the cone to the straw as shown.

**4.** Insert the narrow straw into the wide straw. Hold the narrow straw to your lips at a 45° angle to the ground and blow into it.

3...2...
1...
BLAST
OFF !

Tina Holdcroft

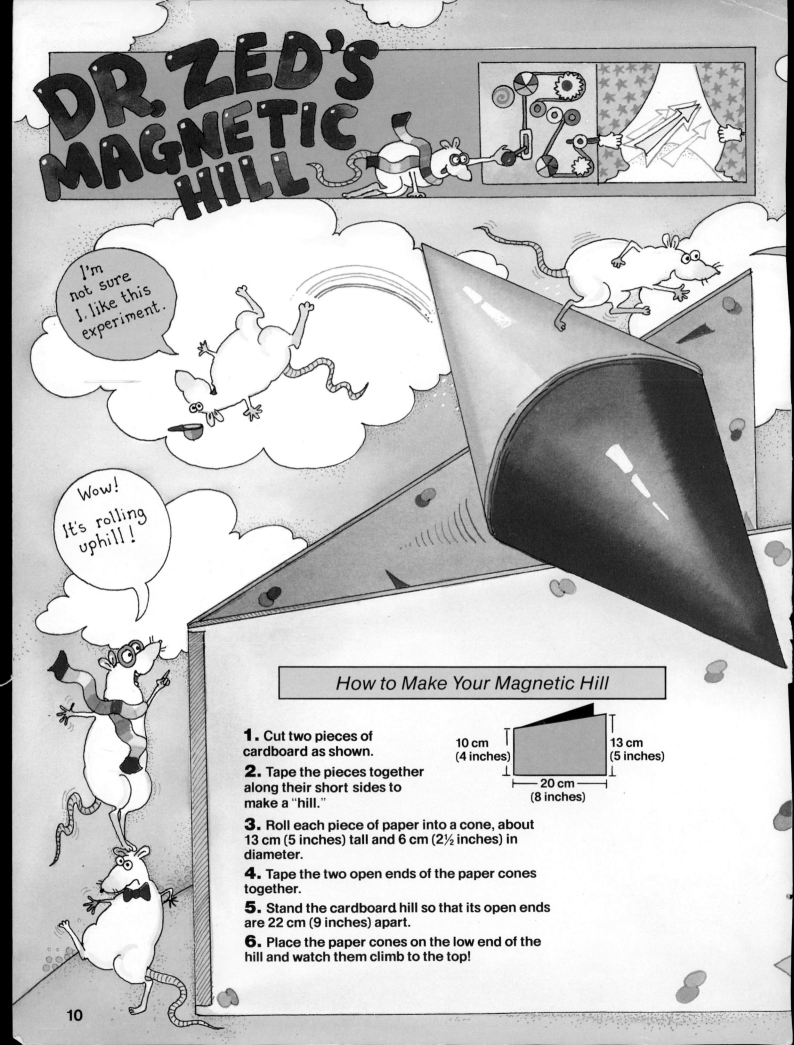

# DR. ZED'S MAGNETIC HILL

I'm not sure I like this experiment.

Wow! It's rolling uphill!

## How to Make Your Magnetic Hill

**1.** Cut two pieces of cardboard as shown.

**2.** Tape the pieces together along their short sides to make a "hill."

**3.** Roll each piece of paper into a cone, about 13 cm (5 inches) tall and 6 cm (2½ inches) in diameter.

**4.** Tape the two open ends of the paper cones together.

**5.** Stand the cardboard hill so that its open ends are 22 cm (9 inches) apart.

**6.** Place the paper cones on the low end of the hill and watch them climb to the top!

10 cm (4 inches)

13 cm (5 inches)

20 cm (8 inches)

11

# DR. ZED'S M-M-MOLECULE MIX-UP

## How to Make Your Molecule Mix-up

**1.** Gather the tools that you'll need: measuring cups and spoons, mixing bowl and spoons, double boiler, four serving dishes.

**2.** Mix together the sugar, cocoa and cornstarch.

**3.** Add the cold water and stir until blended.

**4.** Heat some water in the bottom of the double boiler. Pour the milk into the top. Cook over medium-high heat until the milk just starts to bubble.

**5.** Immediately add the cocoa mixture. Stir constantly until the liquid is thick enough to fall off the spoon in globs instead of running off — it will take five to 10 minutes.

**6.** Add the vanilla, turn down the heat to low and cover the pot. Let the pudding cook for another five minutes.

**7.** Pour the pudding into the serving dishes and refrigerate until cold. Enjoy!

*An adult should supervise your use of the stove.*

12

13

a large plastic container and a small one with a lid; large nail; hammer; nylon stocking; twist tie; 60 cm (2 feet) plastic aquarium tubing; white glue; Perlite or sand; water; houseplant fertilizer; spoon; seeds or seedlings

He's right! Who needs icky soil anyway?

But can you make mud pies out of Perlite?

About this experiment:
Dr. Zed explores the principles of hydroponic gardening.

Soil provides plants with food, water and something to anchor themselves in.

We're giving these plants food dissolved in water and something to anchor themselves in so they don't need soil.

## How to Set Up Your Garden

**1.** Using the hammer and nail, punch a hole in one side of each container, near the bottom. Make another hole in the center of the lid of the smaller container. (When you use the hammer and nail, get an adult to help.)

**2.** Tie a piece of stocking over one end of the tubing with the twist tie. Push this end into the hole in the large container and push the other end into the bottom hole in the small container.

**3.** Make the holes watertight with glue.

**4.** When the glue is dry, fill the large container with wet Perlite and the other one with water. Add a pinch of fertilizer to the water and stir. Put the lid on the smaller container. Place seeds in the large container.

## How to Make Your Garden Grow

**1.** Put your mini-garden in a sunny window.

**2.** Feed your plants once a day by lifting the water container higher than the plant container.

**3.** When the water container is empty, place it lower than the plant container and it will fill up again.

**4.** Once a month add fresh water to the water container until it's almost full, then stir in a pinch of fertilizer.

Yikes! What have you been fed?

Tina Holdcroft

15

# DR. ZED'S ANIMAL KITE

## How to Make Your Animal Kite

1. **String together three straws, then tie them together like this:**

2. **String two more straws together and attach them to the first three like this:**

3. **Thread string through the last straw and attach to the others like this:**

   You've now made a pyramid frame for your kite.

4. **Cover two sides of the frame with tissue paper. Cut the paper big enough so it will wrap around the straws for strength, then glue it to the frame.**

5. **Cut a head and body from construction paper, decorate it and glue it to the frame. Glue on a streamer tail.**

6. **Punch two holes through the construction paper behind the head and near the tail. Cut 25 cm (10 inches) of string to make a bridle and thread it through the holes. Tie each end of the bridle securely around the frame.**

7. **Fasten string to the bridle and... go fly your kite.**

W..w..why do we keep going up, Dr. Zed?

Who's flying this kite?

...Tina Holdcroft...

16

**Things you'll need:**
a container with a flat bottom (a baking sheet works well), milk, food coloring, dishwashing detergent

What's green with red spots?

A pickle with measles!

**About this experiment:**
Dr. Zed looks at hydrophobic (repelled by water) molecules.

Part of each detergent molecule "hates" the water in the milk. The detergent, carrying the food coloring with it, spreads itself over the surface so that the "water-hating" part of each molecule can stick up into the air.

## How to Make Your Exploding Colors

**1.** Pour the milk into the container until the bottom is completely covered.

**2.** Sprinkle drops of food coloring on the milk.

**3.** Add a few drops of detergent in the middle of the largest blobs of color and watch what happens.

19

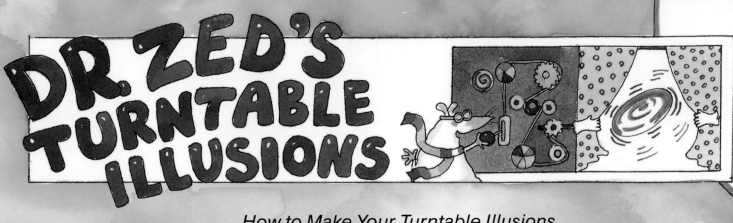

# DR ZED'S TURNTABLE ILLUSIONS

## How to Make Your Turntable Illusions

**1.** Cut a paper circle about the same size as a 45 rpm record and punch a small hole in the middle.

**2.** Draw one of the patterns shown below on your disc.

**3.** Place the disc on your turntable and turn on the turntable as if you're playing a 45 rpm record.

**4.** Watch what happens to the pattern as the disc spins.

**5.** Now try another pattern or make up your own.

# DR. ZED'S PHEWY PUTTY

## How to Make Your Phewy Putty

**1.** Mix together the glue and cornstarch until you can pick up the mixture.

**2.** Work it with your fingers until it's smooth. N.B. Store your Phewy Putty in an airtight container.

22

# DR. ZED'S MAGIC CHECKERS

## Set Up Your Checkers

**1.** Line up six checkers on a smooth table or countertop. Make sure they're in a straight row (a ruler will help) and they should all be touching.

**2.** Place a seventh checker at one end of the line so that there are two checker-widths between it and the end checker.

**3.** Flick the seventh checker sharply towards the end of the line and watch what happens.

Why does only the end checker move, Dr. Zed?

What's that clicking noise?

24

**Things you'll need:**
500 mL (2 cups) flour, 5 mL (1 tsp) baking soda, a pinch of salt, 50 mL (1/4 cup) white sugar, 75 mL (1/3 cup) shortening, 125 mL (1/2 cup) milk, 50 mL (1/4 cup) lemon juice, 50 mL (1/4 cup) chopped red candied cherries

*About this experiment:*
Dr. Zed finds out how a chemical reaction makes tea biscuits rise.

## How to Make Your Valentine Hearts

**1.** Preheat oven to 230°C (450°F).

**2.** Gather the tools that you'll need: measuring cups and spoons, bowl, 2 forks, baking sheet, heart-shaped cookie cutter.

**3.** Mix together the flour, baking soda, salt and sugar. Add the shortening and blend it in by breaking it up with the forks into pea-sized pieces.

**4.** Mix the lemon juice and the milk then pour into the flour mixture. Add the cherries and stir just enough to combine the ingredients.

**5.** Sprinkle a little flour onto a clean counter. Place the dough on the counter and knead it five times. To knead, punch the dough and fold it over.

**6.** Pat the dough until it's about 1 cm (½ inch) thick. Then cut out dough hearts with the cookie cutter.

**7.** Place the dough hearts on the baking sheet and bake for about 10 minutes or until the biscuits are light brown. Decorate and serve them to the one you love. Happy Valentine's Day!

*An adult should supervise your use of the oven.*

# DR. ZED'S TWIRLING MINI-COPTER

## How to Make Your Twirling Mini-copter

**1.** Trace the pattern on this page onto your paper, then cut it out along the solid outside line.

**2.** Cut along line A-B. Fold the wings along the dotted line, as shown.

**3.** Fold the tail along the dotted lines and put the paper clip on the tail, as shown above.

## Flying Your Twirling Mini-copter

Hold your mini-copter, tail down, as high as you can and let it go.

Tina Holdcroft

28

Things you'll need:
paper
pencil
scissors
paper clip

What did one maple key say to the other?

Wanna go for a spin?

About this experiment:
Dr. Zed explores Newton's 3rd law of motion — for every action there is an equal and opposite reaction.

It twirls just like a maple key! But why?

The falling mini-copter only has to turn very slightly for it to set up a movement of air that will keep it twirling.

The mini-copter goes around in the swirling air a bit like a spoon continues to turn in a pot of soup that has just been stirred! ...whew!

Mini-copter pattern

A

Wing                    Wing

CUT ALONG HERE
6 cm
(3 in.)

FOLD    B    HERE

15 cm (1½ in.)

(3 in.)    (½ in.) 1 cm

6 cm

29

Things you'll need:

newspapers; vegetable oil; paper towels; flat aluminum dish; water; thin straws; oil-based paints (model paint works well); a pencil; masking tape; paper or card

About this experiment:
Dr. Zed examines adhesion — the attractive force that works when two different substances are brought into contact.

*Mutter mutter mutter.*

*How was I to know you'd painted the chair?*

## How to Make Your Rainbow Paper

**1.** Spread newspapers on a work surface.

**2.** Lightly oil inside the aluminum dish for easy cleanup. Pour 1 cm (½ inch) of water into the dish.

**3.** Pick up a small amount of paint in a straw. (Thin paint from the top of the jar works best.) Dribble it slowly onto the water.

**4.** Swirl the paint into a pleasing shape with the pencil point.

**5.** Using a different straw for each paint pot, add dots of color to the water, swirling each color as you go. (Try blowing through the straw for an unusual effect.)

**6.** Some paints form a thin skin on top of the water. Remove it with the pencil point as soon as it forms.

**7.** Fasten masking tape loops to the back of a piece of paper. Lift the paper by the loops and gently lay it down on the water. Count to three and pick up the paper by the loops.

**8.** Let the paper dry, paint side up, then remove the loops.

IMPORTANT:   When the paint gets muddy looking, pour it into a container with a tight-fitting lid and ask your parents to dispose of it. **DON'T POUR IT DOWN THE DRAIN.**

*Ahem!
It all has to do with adhesion.
The oily paint is more attracted to the paper than to the water, so it sticks to the paper.*

*Make your lips adhere to mine, ma chèrie !*

31

*It says here that a sowbug is related to a crab.*

*There's not much of a family resemblance is there?*

CRUSTY CRITTERS

**About this experiment:**
Dr. Zed explores the life cycle of the only crustaceans that live on land.

## How to Make Your Winter Home for Bugs

**1.** Layer the jar with vegetation and moist soil, as shown. Put the rock on top of the layers.

**2.** Add a few sowbugs and pillbugs to the jar and cover the top with the towel held in place by the elastic band. Punch air holes in the paper towel.

**3.** Cut the foot off the sock and slide the leg part over the jar to make your "bug" home as dark as possible.

**4.** Check the soil every couple of days. NEVER LET IT DRY OUT.

**5.** If you plan to keep your "bugs" all winter, give them small pieces of lettuce and carrot peelings every few weeks. Put the "bugs" back where you found them after they've had their babies in the spring.

**6.** If you don't plan to keep your "bugs" all winter, put them back where you found them before the cold weather arrives.

*They will mate and the females will carry their eggs around in little pouches.*

*In spring you'll see lots of tiny white babies scurrying around.*

*What happens to them over winter?*

# DR. ZED'S AMAZING ICE CUBE TRICK

## How to Set Up Your Ice Cube Trick

**1.** Ask a friend whether he thinks water is heavier or lighter than oil. Then prove that it's both!

**2.** Fill the jar or glass three-quarters full with cooking oil.

**3.** Gently place the ice cube on the surface of the oil. It will float close to the surface.

**4.** Watch what happens as the ice cube melts. What do the water drops do?

**5.** Can you make an ice cube that's heavier than oil? Try adding food coloring to the water. (Freeze the mixture in a metal ice cube tray since the dye will stain plastic.) How much food coloring can you add before the ice cube sinks?

Things you'll need:
tall jar or glass
cooking oil
ice cube

About this experiment:
Dr. Zed examines what happens as water changes from a solid to a liquid.

What's the hardest thing about learning to skate?

The ice!

... but sink when it melts?

When water freezes, its molecules expand into rigid ice crystals that take up more space than when they were liquid.

Because they weigh the same, they're now less dense than liquid molecules so they float in oil.

··Tina Holdcroft··

35

How to Make Your
Incredible Ice Cream

**1.** Beat the whipping cream until it is stiff.

**2.** Add the other ingredients one at a time, beating mixture after each addition.

**3.** Pour mixture into a small bowl and freeze for two to three hours.

**About this experiement:**
Dr. Zed investigates surface tension (the force that makes a liquid's surface act as if it has a skin).

## How to Make Your Water Tamer

**1.** With the can opener or hammer and nail, punch five small holes near the bottom of the can. They should be about 1/2 cm (1/4 inch) apart, as shown in photo A. (If you use the hammer and nail, get an adult to help.)

**2.** Hold the can over a sink and, covering the holes with a finger, fill the can with water.

**3.** Remove your finger and the water will flow out of the can in five streams. (See photo B.)

## How to Tame the Water

Place your thumb and index finger on the can at either side of the five holes. Pull your finger and thumb towards each other across the holes and pinch the streams together. It's easy to pinch two, three, or four streams so that they combine. But can you tame all five?

39

# DR. ZED'S MAGIC TV STROBOSCOPE

## How to Turn Your TV into a Stroboscope

**1.** Turn on your set, with the volume down.

**2.** Increase the brightness and reduce the contrast to give a bright milky-white screen.

**3.** Now try these experiments.

Things you'll need:
a pencil with an eraser; scissors; sticky tape; thin cardboard; straight pin; ice cream stick

Why did you put a propeller on your clock?

I wanted to see time fly!

About this experiment:
Dr. Zed explores how horizontal and vertical vibrations can be changed to circular vibrations.

## How to Make Your Magic Propeller

**1.** Wrap thin bands of tape around the pencil, adding layers to each band until the pencil looks like this:

**2.** Trace this propeller outline onto the cardboard and cut it out.

**3.** Stick the pin through the center of the propeller, then into the pencil eraser as shown in the photos.

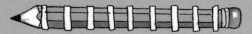

## How to Spin Your Magic Propeller

**1.** Hold the pencil by its pointed end and rapidly rub the stick back and forth along the pencil over the bands. Which way does the propeller turn?

**2.** You can make the propeller spin in only one direction by rubbing your index finger down the length of the pencil while you rub it with the stick. (See the small photograph.) Rub your finger down the opposite side of the pencil to change the propeller's direction.

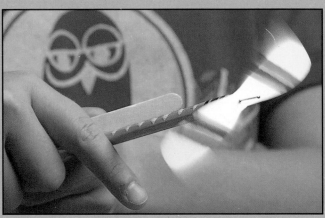

You can also make your propeller by filing notches in the pencil. Get an adult to help.

... and now it's spinning the other way! How does she do that, Dr. Zed?

The stick vibrates the pencil up and down, her finger vibrates it sideways. These motions combine to turn the pencil and propeller in tiny circles. Moving her finger changes the sideways vibrations and the direction of spin.

# DR. ZED'S DANCE-TILL-YOU-DROP POPCORN

What makes the popcorn dance, Dr. Zed?

The baking soda and vinegar react and form bubbles of carbon dioxide. The bubbles attach themselves to the kernels and carry them to the surface. When the bubbles burst at the surface, the kernels sink.

## How to Make Your Popcorn Dance

**1.** Fill the glass with water. Add the baking soda, a few drops of food coloring and stir well.

**2.** Drop in the popcorn kernels then stir in the vinegar.

BAKING SODA

| DATE: | EXPERIMENT: |
| --- | --- |
| | |

NOTES:

# INDEX

## About the Author

Gordon Penrose, the zany Dr. Zed, is regularly featured in OWL, the international magazine for children, and on OWL/TV, the children's discovery program broadcast throughout North America. A retired Master Teacher of Science, Gordon now travels extensively, giving science workshops for children and educators. This is his fifth science activity book.

Dr. Zed's philosophy, like that of OWL Magazine, is that learning can be fun. Because it is important for children to discover for themselves, all the activities in this book encourage creative experimentation, and while each one focuses on one major science understanding, it touches on others as well. All the activities have been tested with children, can be carried out with a minimum of adult supervision, and are designed to be suitable for both home and classroom.